ARRIVAL PRESS

THE PASSAGE OF TIME

Edited by

TIM SHARP

First published in Great Britain in 1997 by
ARRIVAL PRESS
1-2 Wainman Road, Woodston,
Peterborough, PE2 7BU
Telephone (01733) 230762

Copyright Contributors 1997

HB ISBN 1 85786 657 6
SB ISBN 1 85786 662 2

FOREWORD

The Passage of Time is an inspirational collection of verse celebrating the golden years of our lives.

The poets within join together to share with the reader experiences and views on days of old and tales of retirement.

I hope this anthology is a delight to read to all, as I had many enjoyable hours editing it.

Tim Sharp
Editor

CONTENTS

GOLDEN WEDDING DREAMS

We celebrated, every anniversary, John,
    From the first day, that we wed,
With a meal out, or a party,
    Or maybe a holiday, instead.

We were happily married, for forty-two years,
    And tho' we had, our ups and downs,
Your good nature, and your laughter,
    Would wash away, my frowns.

Then seven years ago, we had to part,
    Tho' you fought, so hard, to stay,
But still on our anniversary,
    I celebrate, in my own way.

Next year, will be, our Golden Wedding year,
    And I know, it's something, we can't share,
But I'll still say 'Happy anniversary dear,'
    'Cos I'll pretend, that you are there.

Jean Hendrie

THROUGH EYES OF AGE

A celebration of our age, to husband and to me,
Children grown, flown from the nest, means both of us are free
now to stand, to look at things, before we had no time,
to observe God's wonders which now are partner's and mine.
Deep green fields abound our home, we used to hurry by,
to go to our allotment, we shared one he and I.
Rippling lovely waterways full of roach or trout,
Fishing we'd sit by the edge, or take a boat right out.
Little cottages with thatch, you do not see in town,
Tiny shops where owners let people browse around.
Grey stoned well-built churches, hub of village life,
Sturdy formed farm people, labourer and wife.
We took all this for granted as years went rolling past,
Now our family's grown up, can really look at last.
Farm shops by the roadside, crops straight from the soil.
Prices very low when one considers all their toil.
Age means we're not tied, to rigid scheduled time,
If we're later getting home, there's no one there to mind.
Celebration of age means we are king and queen,
With a royal outlook, our country, all these scenes,
Each day we find new vistas, our eyes now widely see,
Things we took for granted, while raising family.

Barbara Goode

OUR GOLDEN WEDDING DAY

As the years passed our love has grown
Glad times. Bad times we have known
Laughing together drying each other's tears
Loving and supporting through the years

Today it is our Golden Wedding day
When with friends and family we celebrate
A time for reminiscing about times gone by
Now what a contented couple we do make.

Irene Barton

DOWN THE AGES

Age brings a kind of dignity
Unknown amongst the young,
Who, precipitant in action,
And scathing with the tongue.

Age also brings a calmness,
From wisdom years have taught,
Whilst fledglings in their ignorance
Are all to easily 'caught'.

Age knows its place in history,
And the price it's paid
But do the young today
Respect, old sacrifices made?

This 'golden age' - we are told -
But who would want to grow so old?

Sam Stafford

I'D RATHER BE A COWBOY

His head is nodding as he sits in the garden chair
From the stereo inside country music blares
From the outside he may appear to be old
But in his dreams he is young and bold
He imagines himself a cowboy riding western plains
Perhaps holding up a stage for ill-gotten gains
Or fighting the causes of the downtrodden and meek
No longer is he old, feeble and weak
The country western music makes him a child once more
He can be a cowboy hero without leaving his door.

Melanie M Burgess

YOUNG AT HEART

The man leans to his task,
Shoulders bent, stance weary,
White hair blowing in the breeze
As he concentrates.
This same man who once climbed mountains,
Swam with speed and grace,
And survived El Alamein
Now rests a while
Before bending to his work once more.
I watch from the window.
The boy comes eagerly
With his bicycle.
The man takes the bicycle from the boy
Who chatters incessantly
The man answers briefly.
He fetches a tool, and the boy follows,
He returns to the bench, the boy still follows;
The job in hand completed
He passes it to the boy,
And with a gentle cuff
Sends him on his way
The boy replies with mischievous retort
And the man shouts with laughter
Joyous, youthful laughter
It does not matter that he is old,
His spirit is young
He still communicates with youth.

Flora Groves

ONLY A DREAM

The leaves with the breeze gaily flirt
As my aged mind to younger days revert,
To my carefree childhood my memory leans
Ignoring the highs and lows of teenage scenes.

As the dancing leaves their beauty unfold
As a young, happy bride my memory stalled,
And with love my eager mind supplies
A picture of my little ones before my eyes.

But the colourful leaves to me implied
That from my memories I cannot hide;
My life's joys, lost dreams, sadness and pain
Are all linked to life's uncertain chain.

The leaves in sadness their bright colour lost
As on a bed of pain I tossed
Reliving the anguish of the painful past
When my own true love breathed his last.

In pity the good, kind leaves rehearse
A song of love in sweet, tender verse,
And my eager heart on precious memories draw
To hold my own true love once more.

The tired leaves fall gently to the ground
As I prepare for life's last round,
But on the ground they silently weep
For the secret they are sworn to keep.

For they know that it is the scheme
That my life was but a dream,
A dress rehearsal for the gods to ascertain
When I should start to live it all again.

Jean M Shansky

FOR TODAY ONLY

To live in the past
is to live in an ancient
forest, stumbling over
the same old logs,
and, as the future
is not known, it
seems best to live
in the present,
which is all we have,
and not dislike it.

Peter Coxhead

GROWING OLD - DISGRACEFULLY!

When congratulating longevity
It is not the time for levity.
The attaining of countless years of age
When accumulated, now revealing
The ravages of time, not concealing:
A subject in which it's risky to engage.

As a current octogenarian
Of no means outstanding criterion,
I can say, without a shadow of doubt -
My years do not call for celebration:
But maybe today more for condemnation.
Not something I wish to shout about!

Advancing years bring some compensations -
Although short on marital relations.
Still I've discovered there are a few perks:
For instance - time to laze the hours away,
And should I desire - lie in bed all day.
One drawback though. A faulty waterworks!

Jack Judd

OLD

Summer is just a memory.
Autumn lies far behind.
Winter's presence bleak.
Serving only to remind.

My blankets thin and worn.
The fire of life burns low.
The boots are patched.
Fingers gnarled and slow.

A tin of soup on the stove.
But no money for the meter.
A single candle burning low.
Its flame beginning to peter.

But life goes on regardless.
Winter ends, spring slides in.
Summer skies turn blue again.
Until the autumn chills begin.

Edwin W Branagan

THESE AUTUMN YEARS

Autumn is the evening, as a day that's almost gone,
Autumn is the evening of the year.
A comforting season, when now it's time to rest,
Like the day, the summer's gone and peace is here.

Autumn as in life, a retiring time for most,
Resigning from the hard work of the rage.
What bliss to think, and now pause to play the host,
Of the interlude that these autumn years have paged.

Autumn, colours subtle, as the leaves we change our locks,
Not staying as the power of summer's strength.
The beauty of the shades are seen in gentlefolk,
As the sun shines through the leaves in evening's length.

Evenings are the best time, an important part of life,
We can all enjoy the beauty that autumn's brought.
We carpet the world before the wintertime,
Now relax after the summer times are fought.

This gentle autumn fall and the weakening morning sun,
Just waiting for the love that you can give.
And then when night comes and the tranquil day is done,
You will know that this autumn is yours to live.

Lucy-may Bloxham

RETIREMENT

Now I am retired, some say
Over the hill,
I wake up each morning and
Know that I will
Be spared the mad dash to a
Job with no thrill.
Of that kind of life I have
Sure had my fill.

If a club I join is a
Pain in the neck,
I can leave it behind and
Say 'what the heck'.
I am not under contract,
Don't have to stay,
Don't have to fit in. I can
Call it a day.

I can sit in the garden,
Walk by the sea,
Go out to the pub or have
A friend to tea.
Can help out a neighbour with
Mowing, weeding.
At the local school can help
With some reading.

Having friends of like mind to
Share with is grand
But if none are here, on my
Own feet I'll stand.
I can do as I please, don't
Need permission,
Maybe travel the world or
Just go fishing.

Eileen M Ward

MIRROR MIRROR ON THE WALL

I look in the mirror.
Don't like what I see
Grey hairs and wrinkles.
Is this really me?
Where has the girl gone
That I used to be,
With hair dark and curly
And step light and free?
How many years since she tiptoed away
And left me like this
All wrinkled and grey?
The years have rolled by,
But I still feel inside
Young, slim and lissom,
A beautiful bride.

I look in the mirror.
Don't like what I see,
But I cannot deny
That it really is me.

Jess Chambers

FADING

Like summer,
So soft.
The skin:
Now a blend
Of reds and oranges.
The head
Losing leaves.
The feet
Blackened and cold.
The voice
Cackled and quiet to fall.
Like summer.
A mind so swift and clean
Now dirtied by death,
Confused in the draught,
Unable to respond,
To remember with clarity.
You are fading
And in fading
I lose a season
That will never
Shine again.

Matthew Friday

FIFTY

You've reached the age of fifty
It's your birthday just this week
The hair's turning greyer
The bones a little weak

Your mind's a little slower
Take your time at what you do
Middle age spread's occurring
I wonder can you see your shoes

They say when you reach fifty
Your life should travel back
And you must strive to have
All the things life's lacked

When you reach retirement
And you're not sure what to do
Go out and seek new pleasures
Doors will open up for you

G Morrisey

PHEW!

I'd looked forward to retirement.
No more rising at six
Being chivvied by my nursing officer.
Pounding the ward for miles
No more anguish if my patients died
Falling in bed at ten.
Two days off crammed with cleaning.
And shopping and cooking and ironing.
I'd planned a serene time,
Relaxed and free.

So what happened?

Monday - Help at Old People's Centre
Tuesday - Walk the neighbour's dog. Meet friend
              for lunch, tres chic.
Wednesday - Help at Information Bureaux. Meet daughter
              for lunch. Attend art group.
Thursday - Swimming and sauna. Listen to children
              read at school.
Friday - Out with ramblers. 'A' Level at college.

And the other two days?

Crammed with cleaning, and shopping and cooking
                                   and ironing.

And I love it.

Margaret P Derrig

ALTHOUGH I'M GROWING OLD

Although I'm growing very old
and living on my own
I have my Saviour in my heart
so I am not alone.

Although my body may be weak
and folk see me as frail
I have a Lord who strengthens me
each morning without fail.

Although my eyes are getting tired
and not as they should be,
I have God's Spirit in my soul
and truths that I can see.

Although I cannot do some things
that I once did before
God lifts me up on eagles' wings
and in His arms I soar.

Although my stairs are very steep
and shops seem far away
God gives far more than I require
or ask for every day.

How rich I am! I have my Lord
and everything I need.
A Lord who will not let me go.
Yes, I am rich indeed!

John Christopher

FROM A FIT OAP
CONSIDERING OTHERS, TOO

It you're aged and still quite fit; get around
There are pensioner groups to suit you;
With talks; trips; hobbies and shows
Something to suit all of you.

If you're frail, in a home, and can't get around
Without even a stick aiding you
Be willing to let staff take you out in a chair;
Blossoms and blooms around, and you feel the fresh air.

Whatever your state in old age;
Take an interest; keep that old boredom out
Reminisce about your childhood
Others will compare with their own, without doubt.

Tell of your grandchildren
And their chatter and lively air,
They keep your spirits alive
And you like their joys to share!

Speak of your career; of the friends that
                                    you once had.
With chatter and friendly ways
Nothing ever seems quite so bad!

Marjorie Cowan

THE PASSAGE OF TIME

Steadily moving, the passage of time, slowly
maturing like late summer wine.
Each year that ends turns another life page, do we
grow older or just come of age.
The truth surely is we find our true self, as gradually
we store the past on the shelf.
All of life's pleasures we learn to enjoy, relaxing
and leaving the young to be coy.
If there had been choices with what we know now.
I don't really think we would change things somehow.
Life for us all has many ups and downs, but if we
are honest, with more smiles than frowns.
Now when we look back and savour it all, there
are so many fond memories easy to recall.
The seeds of love planted so long ago, have
spread far and wide, but continued to grow
Our families cared for nurtured and fed, bring
forth their beauty like a lovely rose bed.
Their life's just like a garden, we've all had our weeds,
but look what pretty flowers have grown from the seeds.
Time now to harvest and reap our reward, a bounty
of love for working so hard.
As we sit now and take in the evening sunshine,
we have cause to celebrate the passage of time.

Veronica Black

STUBBORN
(For G H)

You said, old lad, the body knows
when it has had enough, and shows

it's time to go. Bones ache, joints creak,
heart flutters, bladder starts to leak.

Well, I can take a hint - no fun
to linger when the race is run.

A decent guest will not outstay
his welcome; best be on your way.

Yet, though we soon must 'come to dust',
still stirs an untamed antic lust

for life - within this husk I find
a curious enquiring mind . . .

Senile I may be, but I crave
a bit more light this side the grave.

Kenneth Wadsworth

MARCH 1942

March 1942 I reached the age of 21
Wasn't a good time, wasn't any fun
Everything was rationed, nothing to bake
No candles to blow out, no birthday cake
Just another day, no celebration
Fighting a war for the peace to the nation
Work it was as usual, to the factory I went
Greetings from mates they were heaven sent
It was my special day but the war didn't stop
Day of hard work until ready to drop
Had a few presents, the nicest I had
A lovely silver watch from my Mom and Dad
I treasured that watch for many a year
Finally it wore out no longer is it here
Remembering that day in 1942
I've blown out candles since, between me and you.
Over the years I've had time to think
My 21st and not even a 'drink'.

Joan Jeffries

HAPPY BIRTHDAY

Seventy is the prime of life,
You've reached it without bother,
Dear Uncle Don it seems to me
It far outweighs all other.

You're fit and well with rosy hue,
All parts in working order,
Friends and family all love you,
Your back could not be broader.

You're kind and soft and do a lot
For others, ever willing
To do good turns and bend an ear
And lend more than a shilling.

So *happy birthday* Uncle dear,
With many more to follow
And don't forget when drinking toasts -
Your legs are not both hollow!

Paddy Jupp

A CELEBRATION AGE

It's a wonderful time
So many things to do
Things you always have
Wanted to do
But did not have
Time
Friends to see
Trips to go on to see
More of the world
To get up when you
Like
Oh it is a wonderful
Time
Of your life
There is joy and
Happiness in our
Hearts
For Celebration Age
So raise your
Glasses.

Eileen Kisby

A 100TH BIRTHDAY

She looks so frail in the big armchair
Bright eyes still very much aware.
Of all the people milling round
But her ears do not relay the sound
Many flowers, a telegram too
Scarves and shawls in vivid hue
So many faces beam and smile
She shuts her eyes to rest awhile
She thinks of all the passing years
Of all the joy and all the tears
A husband, handsome, strong of hand
Who fought in some forgotten land
And babies dressed in pink or blue
All grown up now, and ageing too.
Eyes open now 'What can this be?
So many people here with me'
'Now come on Gran, are you awake?
It's time to cut your birthday cake!'

Joy Nichols

COMING OF AGE

A fly on the wall of your bathroom
Might relate a tale or two
Like the restorer you massage your scalp with
Where a youngster's hair once grew.

It might mention the welts round your middle
False teeth submerged to lift plaque
Or the gasping grunts as you search for your toes
While a disc slips loose in your back.

That face which once overcame pimples
Now has skin the colour of sage
It's all part of an unstoppable process -
Called the second coming of age.

M Devereux

NINETEEN NINETY EIGHT

In January I will be seventy five
I think myself lucky to be alive
I joined the army in nineteen forty two
At eighteen it seemed the right thing to do
I became a sapper, or Royal Engineer
I learnt about bridges, and mines to lay or clear
I was sent to Italy in July forty three
And took part in the invasion of Sicily
Then right thro' Italy, it took nearly two years
When the war ended we were almost in tears
In 1944 Lady Astor said we had dodged D-Day
What did she think we were doing night and day
We were in Europe a long time before then
A lot were killed, who were still young men
We moved to Austria, a nice place to be
And were near a lake called Worthersee
I got demobbed in the bad winter of forty seven
And slept in a bed, it seemed like heaven
It is now fifty-odd years since the end of the war
At times I reminisce about what I did and saw.

George Woollard

SOLDIERS

Where have our handsome soldiers gone,
heroes of long ago.
I see them now with greying hair
and bodies we don't know.

No longer do they stand erect
nor look down at their feet.
As years advance they puff and groan
Where did their ardour go?

But life goes on. We cannot rush.
We stand there on the brink.
They still have glitter in their eyes
whilst we stand at the sink.

The memory remains in mind.
It's all we have you see.
How great those lovely men once were
when we were young and free.

Doris E Pullen

SHELTERED MOMENTS

Day draws to a close
Events fold, time slows
Outdoor activity mellows
Night sets in
Reflect with facial grin
Peace necessary sought
Sheltered moments caught.

Alan Jones

AGE

As we get older and sit side by side
Sometimes words are never spoken, afraid of our reactions
As feelings deep inside never to be broken
Our thoughts of gone-by-days memories good and bad.
Held within ourselves as feelings once we had.
Love for the young now is so quick and gone.
Whereas we older people show love as a much
                                    stronger bond.
Feelings held within never to let go
Smiles upon our faces of years to come not showing
                                    our tales of woe.

Leig

LEST I FORGET

How I wish I could return, again to childhood days,
To see my friends, just as they were, when as a child at play.
To see again that narrow street, the house that we called home,
The milkman with his two-wheeled cart, the cry of 'Rag and Bone'
To hear the sound of ball-race wheels, our wooden scooters made,
Safely in our carefree world, the fun-packed games we played.
To watch a steam train chug its line, and ice-cream from a barrow,
Buy drinks and chestnuts from a stall, that warms you to the marrow.
So many things come flooding back, in that land of yesteryear,
My memory fades, lest I forget, my heart will keep it there.

Thomas Victor Healey

KEEP SMILING

I'm such a happy person, I'm smiling all the time
I have a lot to smile about 'cause everything's just fine.
My family is lovely, I've children I adore
The great grandchildren specially, I hope there'll be some more.
There was a time I could not smile, when I lost my lovely man
But all the happy memories have helped to cheer me on.
Friends I have a-plenty, some old and many new
But real close ones, most have gone, of them there's just a few.
I love to spend my time outside, my garden's wonderful
The trees, the shrubs and plants are all so colourful.
I smile when I look all around, it cheers me up no end
To see the flowers grow so well as each in turn I tend.
Remembering who gave me what, so many years ago
Makes light of the hard work it takes to keep it all just so.
Though I am old, I carry on just as I've always done
I hike and bike and dance and have a lot of fun.
My biggest thrill and widest grin comes when people guess
My age, and nearly always, come up with ten years less.
So I've a lot to smile about, I hope I can keep going
And that at the Millennium I'll be up and doing.
Keep smiling is my motto, ignore the aches and pains
Live for the day, be happy when the sun shines or it rains.

Lisa Wolfe

THE TURNING OF THE TIDE

I may be more forgetful, but I take it in my stride
The kids think I'm going senile, but I take them for a ride
It suits me sometimes, to act vague, I get away with things
That in my youth I never could, a perk that ageing brings
I always played the actress, but this is my favourite part
After all life's joys and dramas, I know the lines by heart
My deafness is a burden, especially on the phone
But I use it like a party trick, when I want to be alone
It's amazing what they talk about, thinking I can't hear
I watch their lips so carefully, the message loud and clear
They think I'm so eccentric, surrounded by my cats,
And herbs and psychic interests, not to mention all my hats
I no longer set out to impress, with all the latest gear
My only complaint in my sixties - shop girls who call me 'Dear'
I have no wish for youth again, with all its stress and strife
I take each day now as it comes and go with the tide of life
For the tides are always turning, they ebb and then they flow
And now my high tide has been reached who knows where
                                                    I will go!

Gwendolyn Cameron

A CELEBRATION OF AGE

I was born the year *nineteen twenty eight.*
Every day a celebration till I was *five*
And now my mother is not alive.
At *six* I was taken over by the State
In a home for soldiers' daughters when I was *eight.*
I talked and had tea with Royals who have been
                                    upon the throne
A celebration not everyone has known
The next *eight* years have flown.

At *seventeen* I am free
I have to look after me
I dance and sing the days away, a happy heart
Eighteen, England calls me to do my part
I toil and dig with fork and spade
At *twenty* become a nurse's aid.

For many years in lodgings I did reside
At *twenty-five* I became a bride
To my sorrow he had no manly graces
He did not give me love and embraces
My love I gave, and at *twenty seven*
A little girl, a gift from heaven
Such joy to help me through my sorrow
So I can face each tomorrow

At *forty-five* I shed the gold band
Someone else to take my hand, a celebration it was grand.
My daughter now is leading lady on the stage
I need a champagne, *forty-nine* is now my age.
A grandson at *fifty-five*
It is so great to be alive
At *fifty-eight* a grand-daughter so small
And she is cherished by us all.

Sixty, a pension book arrived to say
Fifteen pounds for Christmas was on its way
At *sixty-five* I'm still here
Singing to over five hundred on a square in Mere
Now at *sixty-nine* I feel fine
A celebration on the PO Line
I was old when I was young,
Now I'm old, spring has sprung.

Kathy Paris

DEPRESSING BUT TRUE

Old age is depressing it has to be said
Up early in the morning, then early to bed.
The day is spent thinking of what might've been
One fact of life, our future is no dream.

When you get older and your mind starts to slip
It's just the beginning of this old-age trip.
Your joints start to ache, you don't like to complain
You know deep down, you'll never be the same again.

There must be some good to be old and wise
To have good health and to tell no lies
Some people say she's bitter, twisted and old
It's just possible they might be as good as gold.

Amanda Sullivan

THANKSGIVING FOR DAYS PAST AND FUTURE

How glad I am that time remains
To savour life at last.
Since happy, sad, and busy times
Have jostled in the past
With aims and goals
And problems.

There has been no time to stand apart
And ponder on my fate.
It has seemed inevitable
That I should live in that state.
The time has come
To reflect.

What has been the pattern?
Should I change it now.
I am already pulling
Life's threads together. This is how
to feel fulfilled,
Satisfied.

Aims achieved and goals attained,
It is time to assume
Enjoyable experiences
Are yet to come. A blessing
For the future.
Now give thanks.

Janet Wason

A Word From The Wise

Isn't it strange how age through the ages
Constantly writes ever longer pages
In ancient times we scarce wrote a few lines
yet today each life is a novel of our times
And family events are duly recorded
Some to be celebrated, some sadly, sordid
And life goes by as if in a race
The older you get, the faster the pace
Till now, through age, you are one of the wise
Who knows all the answers to everyone's whys
Or so the younger will say they believe
When a problem's answer they cannot conceive
But this is the time for each erudite sage
To turn one more adventurous page
For with children grown and grandchildren growing
Now is the opportunity for you to be going
To attempt all ambitions held through the years
And carry them through regardless of fears
Since science has improved our expectations of health
And the added years have increased our wealth
So age is a time we should really enjoy
And not remain anchored to some inshore buoy
Just cut all the ropes, remove all the traces
Go out in the world and visit those places
That formerly were merely the focus of dreams
Will become reality as you can say 'I've been!'

Richard Hallewell

MARCH OF TIME

Countless days and years have gone
As time weaves its tragic spell
Playing tricks with the body
Tampering with the mind as well

Youthful looks have disappeared
The hair is thin and greyed
Skin looks like an old road map
And everything else has strayed

The march of time has taken its toll
It makes me feel a little slow and lazy
Forgetting things I ought to know
Sometimes it drives me crazy

I know that it's just a frame of mind
And that there's really no need to fear
But the ageing process continues
I get the same feeling every single year

I know that I should be happy
Well that's what my friends say
But it does seem to get a little harder
With each passing birthday

Roy Hunter

MASTERPIECES

My wife brought home a tape from one of her old fellas
she placed it in our machine
and this old guy began to talk about life
and how he had been giving life a lot of thought just lately
Stuff about stock-takes
what we do with our lives and
what we can do.
Now I didn't know much about Donald or what he had done
apart from paint his late wife in the nude
but I listened and the old man's dream became clear:
to write a great novel
a manuscript
or paint a masterpiece to hang in a gallery
something to live on after him, leave his mark.
How did he put it? Leave a tip in the restaurant of life
that was it, and here he was
almost ninety.
Anyway, he got onto words and his lifelong love affair with them
eventually getting into his poems.
Don't, said my wife
What?
Laugh.
But I wasn't laughing
She was embarrassed now, listening with me there
uneasy, afraid I would say something cruel
You don't have to listen to this, why don't you go for your bath?
And so I did
From the bathroom I heard her occasional chuckle
Doesn't he have a nice voice? He's such a lovely man
He was so pleased when I said I'd like to listen to his poems
She laughed but when I looked down her face was sad

He's so determined. So much he must give up
Tears in her eyes
I take my hat off to him, really I do
as she leaned to turn off the tape.

Mark Renney

AGE UNCONCERN

Retirement beckons
My body reckons
It's time to stop
A race to the top

Better by far
To follow my star
Relax and enjoy
Life's every joy

So I'll accept limitations
Adjust to frustrations
Spend time on myself
Content on my shelf.

S Lee

I REMEMBER

In dreams I still see faces whose names are lost to me
from the distant days I've left behind,
the images of school friends, once so close to me,
in the silence of the night return to mind.

I remember carefree summers spent playing by the sea,
and winters when the air was crisp with snow
how we wandered far and wide, without a trace of fear,
in the safety of a world we used to know.

I remember my first boyfriend, and his strong and handsome face,
how when dark clouds gathered he left our little town,
later he was listed among the heroes of our time
who sacrificed their youth on battlegrounds.

I remember how I cried at first, then moving on I saw
A different post-war world before my eyes,
The homes we loved were flattened to make way for other things,
like superstores and tower blocks to rise.

We learnt a different language of computer codes and skills,
we saw Europe reborn and watched the Empire fade,
we knew that things were better and our lives improved
but despite those comforts, sometimes we are afraid.

Still in the darkest hours, I can quietly recall
all those friends and family who were so dear to me,
and be happy in the knowledge that, no matter what they change,
no thief can ever steal away my precious memories.

Ann Rutherford

THE OLD VICAR

He had always worn black
(Harrods, maybe, hand-tailored)
too big for him, the creases
unnaturally resistant
to the small body wriggling within.
The long stiff neck -
scrawny or scrannel -
he always loved a textual crux -
I most remember, magic
of Adam's Apple reciprocating
like a plunger in a white wheel
unbroken by spokes,
the shining silk full stock
('breastplate of righteousness'
we used to call it),
the dazzling collar window
two inches by regulation one,
the ample crossed seated pants
in which thin buttocks
jostled like big potatoes.

Wasting away, he was the same
only more so - the wintry blue smile
exposing and releasing dental rot;
the cheeks, scattered with red-
veined filaments, grew snow-white
whiskers mollified by age.
He stooped with years
and laughed more often
with a sad clear vacancy
redolent of dementia.
But he was invulnerable.
His faith was incontinent -
it knew no bounds.

He sank like a russet into his chair,
the sun of hope imparting a blossom,
as he basked in the certainties of belief
whilst we jealously prepared
for the turmoil of grief.

Eric Smith

HERE WE ARE

There we were,
A new union;
Blessed by the Church;
Accepted by the State,
Otherwise - we were on our own.

There we were,
With our assets pooled;
Blessed with one room;
Accepted - with one case.
Other things - little of our own.

There we were,
Our daughters now born;
Blessed with a flat;
Accepted for HP.
Other joys - loved ones of our own.

There we were,
The girls in their teens;
Blessed with a house;
Accepted for mortgage.
Otherwise - little time of our own.

There we were,
The girls flown from the nest;
Blessed with our work;
Accepted our new role.
For others - gave time of our own.

There we were,
Now in retirement;
Blessed with good health;
Accepted good fortune;
Toured other countries than our own.

Here we are,
Grandchildren grown up;
Blessed with our love;
Accepting age with grace.
Each other - the wealth of our own.

Roy Hammond

SILVER, GOLDEN AND DIAMOND

Anniversaries to celebrate
On life's journey at each stage,
Silver, Golden and Diamond
Come with endurance, love and age.

Twenty-five years becomes our Silver
A time to recall, reflect,
Memories that we have shared
That come with love and warmth, respect.

Fifty years to rejoice and Golden
An achievement with a bow,
Our sacred binding promise
And a renewal of our vow.

Sixty years is our precious Diamond
With splendour, sparkle and shine,
On this stage of our journey
We give our praise and thanks combine.

These celebrations with thanksgiving
On a journey with review.
Silver, Golden and Diamond
Shine best when love and hearts are true.

Peter James O'Rourke

APPRAISING

We could be Church of England
But not so well defined
Mix with voracious marriage flocks
Kneel in the pews around the box
Religiously inclined.

Do we believe the virgin birth
That church disciples say
Resort to Sunday hymns of praise
Canonical in all our ways
Or spiritually pray?

The witnesses have stayed away
No Watchtower ever bought
They all perceive we doubt a lot
And though we never shout a lot
We often feel we ought.

Surrounded in our eloquence
Do we conceal our fears?
No poverty surrounding us
No church dictates are grounding us
Inhibiting the years.

So maybe we should hedge our bets
The cards are marked and dealt
Old age is bound to gravitate
And by then it may be too late
For heaven to be felt.

Clive W MacDonald

A Celebration Of Age

Sitting cosily, in her armchair,
100 years old today is Claire.
She can't see too well and her hearing has gone,
but she happily sits there, singing a song.
Her family are helping her to celebrate,
with a glass of wine and cream cake on a plate.
She may have no teeth, but she still tucks in
and is even asking for a gin!
So many cards have arrived for Claire,
her celebrations, they all want to share.
The Queen, also wished her a happy day;
A celebration of age? What more can I say?

Ruth Gatenby

MILESTONES OF LIFE

The birth of a child, a miracle of life,
The first steps, the first words.
School with its pleasures and strife,
Where we're taught 'bout the bees and the birds.
The first teenage years
With its joys and its tears,
The first love affair, but is it right?
Time will tell if a marriage is in sight.
The walk down the aisle as your new wife,
Our first anniversary, one of many.
The cycle starts again, we're blessed with new life,
The struggles to make a pound from a penny.
The Silver Wedding, 25 years on.
The Ruby, 15 years later,
Then comes the Golden but alas, you are gone,
Back to the Maker, our very own Creator,
I'm left with memories sweet and bad,
But there is still one celebration
The very last one of all,
At the end of life's duration
When I answer the angel's call
And rejoin you once and for all.

Rose E E Thurley

THE ZIMMER FRAME

There's a zimmer in the attic
We bought it for our mum,
Once she got used to using it
She moved - just like Red Rum!

She zimmered round the house with it
She zimmered down the street,
It gave her back her freedom,
It gave her back her feet.

And now its job is over,
Our mum has passed away
So the zimmer's out of action
Until another day.

Pamela R Pickford

MOBILITY

Mobility, mobility, there's nothing like
mobility,
To walk around, to run around, with
unimpaired agility.
I had this power when I was young, this
marvellous facility.
I took it all for granted then, as
natural ability.

But with the years my legs have lost
a lot of their virility.
The unrelenting march of time has lessened
their utility
Or as they say in USA, 'Reduced their
capability.'
I hope there'll be no worsening, but
'medical stability'.

The trouble has not reached my mind or
thoughtful sensibility
And up to date I don't expect incipient
senility.

In dreams some nights I walk again, but
day brings disability.
I try to face my present state with
imperturbability
And with an inner sense of peace, and
humour and tranquillity,
Rejoicing that my mind is free, to range
with real mobility.

Norman Hurst

YET ANOTHER BIRTHDAY

Now that you've turned yet one more page
In life to reach that ripe old age
Of three score years and thirteen too
Which is just one more than seventy-two.

Be careful how you live your life
By not doing things that cause you strife.
In fairness try to shed your load
While travelling down life's busy road.

Be kind to those who love you true
Who think of things for them to do
To take the strain from off your mind
For another you would be hard to find.

Gerard Oxley

APPLE GRANNY

Granny always did love apples
Therein lay her curse
Her appetite would not abate
But with her years grew worse
The crisp young apple's flesh once bitten
Could now be only sucked
Whilst rosy reds whose juices dripped
From memory she plucked

Her craving seldom satisfied
By apples baked with spice
Granny felt so cheated
With the cooking's softened price
She yearned for something firm and fruity
Something with a kick
To tickle her old tastebuds
And that would not in gullet stick

Then lo! In answer to her prayers
One night came Scrumpy Jack
He swept her off her feet
And to her youth he took her back
She frolicked with him 'til the stars
Looked near enough to touch
Gambolling through the summer meadows
Memory still clutched.

Kim Montia

DIAMONDS

We've been together for all of sixty years,
Through good times, and times full of fears.
Time hasn't dulled the love we first knew,
But, that it has grown and matured, is true,
We have a family, a blessing from above
To cement that true and abiding love.
As I look down the years at times gone past,
The good times are the only ones that seem to last.
We had our share of trouble and bother,
But you see, we always had each other,
A trouble is halved, if, a trouble you can share,
have plenty of love, and a little to spare.
To care for each other is the first rule,
And age doesn't cause this love to cool,
It only grows stronger the older we get,
And so the best years are still to come yet.

June H Rogers

UPDATED NOT OUTDATED

Look in your cupboard
And what do you see?
There's a 'use by' date
On everything, even tea!

Look in your fridge.
Don't use things too late;
There's a 'best before' date.
These things make me so irate!

I've looked all over
And cannot find . . .
A 'use by' date on me!
But society says:
At 65 you just cease to be.

We should be stamped,
With a 'best after' date.
We may not be in the best of health.
Please don't take us off the shelf!
We lived a lot; have memories by the score;
Just listen a bit and you can learn more.
Because we're old, we have lots to share,
With younger ones for whom we care.

Rosemary Taylor

AUTUMN TIME OF LIFE

September brings the mellow days,
No need to rush and scurry.
Now there's time to 'stand and stare',
No work day fuss and flurry.

The blessing, once more, of children.
This time the joy without pain.
And knowing that though you love them,
Grandchildren go home again!

Time to potter in the garden,
Read a book from start to end,
Time to have coffee with a neighbour,
Time to write a letter to a friend.

Time to brush up skills forgotten,
To discover talents new.
Go out and seek if you would find,
For the world won't come to you.

Make the most of these, your autumn days,
With the slower pace you'll find
A new enjoyment of your life,
And sweet serenity of mind.

Edna Ridge

INVESTMENT

I saw a vineyard, with each tender vine
Grape clustered, but the harvest was not due.
I spoke to their custodian, who knew
One day they'd make a rich and timely wine.
With friends around my table now, I dine
And open up a bottle, as men do
And reminisce on times both old and new
To celebrate a future which is mine.
For now, like wine, I feel I have matured
Through sun and circumstance which brought me here.
Fulfilment comes with age, I am assured.
I share the substance, rich, full bodied, clear,
The product of my birth, a vintage year.

William Craven

Too Much

My poems are silent quarrels with time
elbowing the rhyme and reasons tense
so no-one would guess we scream
at the end of every line defence
in the hollow swell, the tornado dream
turbulent with discontent, held down
like fighting the time between the town
and quiet life, delight after hurt
the quiet dessert, the plum under the thumb
sweetness under the crumb of comfort done,
there's my love consort and confusion fall
like clothes thrown off in red lust call,
we were to fight, to love, to maul
that we'll remember most of all
the touch, the touch, the touch together
almost . . . too much.

Pam Stanborough

GRAN AND GRANDAD'S ALLOTMENT

In the beginning not much to see,
Overgrown and not worth the fee,
Chop the grass, plant a few seeds,
They'll soon take care of those nuisance weeds,

After it's cleared, good as new,
Don't get me wrong, there's still lots to do
Making the paths to walk along,
Collecting manure (despite the pong!)

At last the strawberries are ready to eat
With a dollop of cream they'll go down a treat,
Sprouts, cabbage, kohl rabi, green beans
Well some people like them, strange though it seems

There's vegetables common, vegetables rare
So all you vandals had better beware
For on the allotment they work as a team
Winning some, losing some, making their dream.

But food isn't all as you enter the gate
it's hello, how do, to all their new mates
Everyone's pitched in and the end result's not half bad
So very well done to my gran and grandad.

Katie Rolfe

WHEN WE RETIRE

When me and my Dutch retire well er
We won't be just sat around
There's so much of life we've yet to discover
So many new sights and sounds

A toast to us for the life ahead
We'll set the world on fire
We'll be just like them there Adamsons
When me and my old lady retire

We'll buy a camcorder between us
And record things for our TV
We're going to go off discovering things
That we've never been able to see

We'll trek for lost temples, down some jungle trail
And have a picnic on the way
We'll see if the female's more deadlier than the male
And we'll wish her a right grand day

We'll canoe through a mosquito ridden rainforest
Cross a croc infested swamp
In search of an elusive tribe of cannibal pygmies.

The rinky dinky donk.
We could snowshoe through the Himalayas
With our Parkas fastened up tight
And stop to chat up a yeti
How you doing cock, alright?

What about home by the fire
With our legs on a stool
Matching slippers on our feet
With our grandchildren telling us all about school
That must be the finest treat.

Fred Tighe

ANCIENT LIGHTS

So they are done, the seventy years
And now the rapid weeks rush
Ever faster to oblivion.
Familiar names more frequently
Announce their leaving in the Telegraph
But as with wartime lists of casualties
My name could be there too,
And isn't. I am fortunate,
All systems working and
So much to savour still.
It does not do to contemplate
The bridge or bridges still to cross
And least of all to think the loss
Of lovely her who means so much.
No, no - for there are grandchildren, and travelling,
Grass to cut, committees, watching shares -
Perhaps tomorrow I'll go through
Those attic boxes, throw away
Some junk, sort out old papers,
Perhaps. There's lots of time. Perhaps.

John Wedge

GROWING OLDER

Growing older, growing older,
Time flies faster every day.
Fun leisure days of younger years
Seem further, further, far away.

Memory plays tricks these days.
It 'isn't what it used to be.'
Names, dates, occasions, muddle up
But I *am* still the same old *me!*

Am I happy? Yes I am.
We've daughter, son, and families,
Friends, food and warmth, and home sweet home.
I truly think we've all we need.

One day that's not so far away
Someone will say 'The time has come,'
To 'Shut up shop' and give up all.
It's just the same for everyone.

M C Cobb

TOGETHERNESS

Like life itself, we too grow old
We pass the time, yet feel the cold
Day comes round, as night time passes
We rise from our bed, and put on our glasses
Once we were so young and fair
Now all we see, is grey in our hair
Our time that's been spent together
Has often left us under the weather
Yet when we reflect, on times gone by
There is no strange reason, we wonder why
We were meant for each other
Just like our folks before,
Our dad and our mother.

Les J Croft

WAITING AT THE STATION

Waiting at the station,
Steam billows all around.
Is my Charlie on the train?
At last homeward bound.
All the horror of that war
Will at last be shed.
Shadowy figure runs into my arms,
Soon we shall be wed.

Waiting at the station,
Diesel leads the train.
See my Charlie at the window,
My loneliness will wane.
Remembering another station,
Anxiety, many fears,
It ended with a union,
Bringing many happy years.

Waiting at the station,
Memories fill the air,
My young man in his demob suit
Bringing love for us to share.
Was it only last year
My Charlie passed away?
This Charlie is my grandson
Bringing happiness to me this day.

Josie Minton

AUTUMN AND MIDDLE YEARS

The days are short,
The shadows long,
In Blewitt Court
The lunchers throng
The steamy caff.

And fifty looms
A year away.
Is autumn gloom
In me today?
I force a laugh.

What's fifty years
In endless time?
Two salty tears?
A nursery rhyme?
Some wind-chased chaff?

What cares are these
How far we've come?
From Eden's trees
Or primal scum
Or aliens' gaff?

So fifty comes
And fifty goes
And what the hell
If fifty *shows!*
No cenotaph
Will mark the flight
Of my small life
Into the night.

David J Ayres

SONNET TO AGE

The Bard has told us that in our long span
There are seven ages in the days of man.
He paints a picture of each scene of life,
Portraying melancholy, tears and strife.
Now I have passed through some of these stages,
Shared joys and sorrows down through the ages.
Approaching soon those three-score years and ten,
And counting blessings in retirement when
In contemplative fashion I recall
Those happy times which God gives to us all.
I don't presume to argue with the Sage,
And his interpretation of each age,
But now I can with calm serenity,
With hopeful heart look to eternity.

Kath Hurley

THE GOLDEN YEAR

Growing up in the age of Elizabeth II, our Queen
Has been a wonderful era and most serene,
Especially for those born in her generation
Who fought or helped to save our nation
So that our descendants would be free,
Then later to marry and start a family tree.

The year 1947 was very special for every young bride to be
Including Princess Elizabeth who walked down the aisle so free
Just 21 years old with Prince Philip on the 8th of November
The wedding of the year and one to be remembered,
And now in nineteen-ninety seven
Their Golden Year which is a gift from Heaven,
To be married and loved for half a century
Is a wonderful achievement for every golden couple's anniversary.

A lot of water has ebbed to and fro under the bridge
During those fifty years and over the ridge
With the ups and downs which were quite unforeseen
For every married couple and the same for Elizabeth now our Queen.
But with God's blessings we are able to cope
Through life's traumas and not to give up hope.

It is nice to remember the happy times and forget the sad
As the years have passed by maybe we are glad,
To be able to celebrate in our own small way and not too downhearted
Or disappointed if we were not invited to the Queen's Golden Party.
Instead happily joining in with friends and relations
Wishing Her Majesty and everyone hearty congratulations.

May the years ahead be trouble free
With good luck and traditional legendary,
We pray for peace all over the world
Hoping the problems will soon be unfurled,
When everything will perhaps be reduced to a minimum
As we look forward to the future and the millennium.
Now in the last decade of the twentieth century
May God Bless every Golden couple and long live the Monarchy.

Nancy Owen

CELEBRATION OF AGE

We're yesterday's men of tomorrow,
For we're halfway down the track,
With the hope of youth and the strength of age,
Like Janus, look forward and back.

We dug the coal and built the ships,
And we made the best steel as well,
We showed them all we led the world,
And, Oh what a tale we can tell.

We've seen a lot and done a lot,
We've seen the trams go rattling by -
Now hear the jets come screaming in,
The 'wild night riders' of the sky.

From red flags and the motor car,
To the rocket that's off to Mars.
From crystal set to compact disc
Is there life on one of the stars?

It's a story without ending,
The hi tech flows in like a tide,
We've seen so much as life flows on,
Yes, we take it all in our stride.

John Horton

SILVER COIN

Breeding in a new world -
I spread my wings.
Flying into the sunrise
No-one can touch a bod
So wondrous in the new dawn . . .
I have no ties.

Greenlands which I can brush
Just like a feather stroking my skin.
Should I pass over a dark angel -
I'll fight a battle so strong
Shadows will avoid me
Every creature will begin to hush.

The sky begins to darken
It is time for me to wonder,
Over a journey that
Never took a lifetime to plan -
Yet took years to begin.
Look at me now -
Mature but breathless.
Look at my new tattered hat.

So is new knowledge to be learnt
From someone like me?
Perhaps you should ask:
Then plan your own journey.

Jagdeesh Sokhal

PLUS ÇA CHANGE, PLUS C'EST LA MÊME CHOSE

Each succeeding day brings something new.
A trite and empty saying? I think not.
We spend our early years acquiring
The trademarks of the age in which we live.
The contrast with our parents' homely goods
Points up the seemingly abiding joy
Of innovation and improved design.

As the years pass we observe the changes
Wrought by the young ones on their daily lives.
We see the hankering for innovation
As a tiny part of in-built search
For the unattainable perfection;
That little spark of our earthly self
Struggling within a very earthly body
To attain its goal.

With this realisation comes contentment.
We no longer focus on surroundings,
But turn these energies to gratitude,
To efforts for the world beyond ourselves,
To realisation that the timeless search
For ultimate perfection will be granted
In no material way.

It's wholesome to rejoice in evolution,
To recognise the part it has to play
In satisfying man's creative urge,
His building and developing of talents;
But we must be aware of subtle barriers
Between our genuine needs and the temptation
To replace sound and serviceable items
With novel but still transient acquisitions.

K Maureen Inglis-Taylor

SANS EVERYTHING!

Gone are the golden locks of yore,
and teeth sit in a mug -
my second 'eyes' are trusty friends -
and waistbands need a tug!
What once I used to do with ease
with no thought given to,
now takes me half a day, no less,
and energetic days are few!
I must admit, I'm growing old,
my 'oats' are long since sown,
and when I 'youthful' try to be
I'm whacked, laid-out, and *blown!*
So now I'm just content to sit
when my normal chores are done -
(I must admit it tires me out
just *watching* others having fun!)
And, if something's said
I'd lief not hear -
what good excuse! -
my failing ear!
Because I'm old, I'm waited on
by family and by friends,
and should I say something 'not on' -
I pathetic look, and make amends!
The internal machinery rusty grows
with age, that is a fact of life,
so, all the strenuous, demanding
things, I shamelessly leave - to my wife!

Joyce Hockley

JUBILATIONS

As I recall the days gone by
Tears, happiness and joy
Hard work and apprehension
Of life's incessant ploy
I count my present blessings
On fingers of four hands
To have you still around me
In spite of trickling sands
Photos all around the walls
A pot of tea we share
We wallow in the ecstasy
Of our love in cosy lair
I care for you, you care for me
A celebration true
Age cannot dim our constant love
That grew and grew and grew . . .

Louise King

BROKEN DREAMS

When I reached fifty
I promised myself
a new look and partner
not to be left on the shelf.
But instead I gained weight
despite several diets
and a creative coiffeur
I prefer to keep quiet.
No more travel to countries abroad,
once taken for granted
but cannot afford.
My children have problems
and fill me with pain,
no wish to traverse the
path that I came.
Nature and home are all I require
or the heavenly sound of a church choir.
Familiar faces, an occasional treat,
home comforts, good health are still
hard to beat.
So I try to accept my standard of living,
after all the years of loving and giving.

B J Harrison

FIFTY

Reaching the age of fifty
Isn't all that bad
If you haven't already got memory loss
You'll remember the good years you've had
I'm sorry 'bout the wrinkles
And the crows' feet round your eyes
This happens when skin gets thin and old
They are things that you just can't disguise
Receding, greying hairline, expanding middle-age spread
So long as this all continues
You will know that you're not dead!

Janette Harazny

I AM BLESSED

I look back at my life
A smile on my face
The friendships I made
Not forgetting a face
The places I travelled
The sights I have seen
I conquered it all
Fulfilled every dream.

My children, all happy,
Their children too,
Home comforts surround me,
Out of my window,
A postcard view,
The good times, they easily,
Outweigh the bad,
It seems I've always been
happy,
Very rarely sad.

So as I lay in my bed
Surrounded by lace
I laugh out loud at the
reflection of my face,
My smile in a glass
My eyes in their box
My ears wrapped up neatly
next to my clock.
I may have grown old
My lines may have crept,
But this face is a loved face,
And I know I am blessed.

Caroline Kinnear

WINDS OF LIFE

Blow morning wind from the dawning east,
fresh and dew laden, sweeping away
the shades of night, the cloud of doubt,
the web of dreams, and let the hopeful ray
of new day bring enlightenment to the problems of reality.

Blow midday wind from the distant north,
icy sharp, letting your keen tang breathe
cool reason into the troubled heart,
soothing hot passions and hatreds, turning them
to zestful energy for the fulfilment of hopes.

Blow noontide wind from the sun washed south,
warm and gentle, sweetly scented, giving
balmy airs to ease the weary limbs that have laboured
to achieve that of which they cannot know the right or wrong,
but only know they worked for it in good faith.

Blow evening wind from the sunset west,
bringing the breath of dear loved moorlands,
tinting the sky with softly blended shades of memory
and I will know, when my work is done, that tomorrow
will dawn once more though I may not wake to see it.

For as I would be born to the east wind,
work with the north wind, rest under the south wind,
so 'tis in the west wind that I would die
and let tomorrow's winds make what they will
of my life's effort. Only let them bear in mind
that I did, even as they will believe they do,
the best I could, within the limits of my vision.

Jean Collins

LOSSES AND COMPENSATIONS

The day has come to bid all your work colleagues a sad farewell
The many years of work have come to an end, and truth to tell,
You have such mixed feelings as you look back over your past
It's good to feel free from the alarm clock and struggle to work at last
But you fret over those unfulfilled ambitions you had when you
were young
But cheer up, the song of life has not yet been completely sung
You may have some wrinkles, your skin is not quite so glowing
and taut
Joints are less supple, movements slower, but here is a
cheering thought
Your family has been reared, now is the time to indulge yourself
Pamper and treat yourself with your hard earned 'wealth'
Without the demands of work to eat up all your energy and time
Take up painting, pottery, languages, put your thoughts into rhyme
Now you have more time to chat to friends and neighbours, even
your husband
Even to go to the seaside and, like a child again, make sandcastles
in the sand
In the cocksure days of youth everything is seen in black and white
Now you can see the other's point of view and see that maybe
he is right
The mind may not be quite so quick, but ideas are backed up by
maturity
You are less quick to lose your temper, your face is lit by a
new serenity
Eat a healthy diet, exercise your body, and exercise your mind
And with a little wise planning, and some luck, you may well find
That the best years of your life are yet to come, enjoy what lies ahead
Don't think that just because you leave the bustle of work you are
as good as dead
All that you have been, and done, these many long years make you
A special person in the community to whom respect is surely due

You have come through the demands of life and played your useful part
Now give time to yourself, now at last you may finally start
To stop pushing aside your dreams, allow yourself your full worth
Celebrate age, and make the most of the rest of your time on earth.

Margaret Meagher

TOGETHER

Some say the secret of long life is healthy living -
abstinence from fags, alcohol, rich food, and the dreaded
cholesterol. Others believe it is genetic, that we are
what our ancestors make us. While further schools
of thought adhere to a philosophy that embraces
a calmness of mind, taking life as it comes in a
non-frenetic way; that not giving in to rage, and keeping
the blood pressure steady, paves the way to a serene
old age. Keeping oneself active is said to prevent
decline; mind and body need gentle, regular workouts
to prevent premature decay. I simply don't know;
all I can say is this - that I shall live just as long
as fate decrees; and that I want to spend the years
I have left with you, being loved, and irritated,
and enraged by you, as I have for the last thirty years.
And I know that I speak for you, (though you'd never
put the Great Unspeakable into words), when I add
that every year has been a celebration; that we've
no intention of changing the status quo; that our time
together has been rich and rare; that the one without
the other would be quite lost; and that whichever one of us
breathes the last will count the greatest cost.

J M Service

THE LAST SYMPHONY

The old man's life is at an end,
All storms subsided,
Everything is in the past;
Now, nature weeps in his stead,
He has no more tears left to shed;
Waits in gloomy shadows like a wreck,
His story told to many a young man,
His experiences over, but well spent.

Raymond Fenech

OLD! - NOT ME

A pensioner! - I guess I am
I might be in a state
Short-sighted - arthritic and creaking joints
And past my sell by date.
And then my little grandson
Comes bounding on the scene
Excitedly telling me what he's done
The places he had been
Then it's 'Come on nanny - get up'
Let's play 'footie' on the green.
Then off to the park for a session
of swings and slides and such
And the daunting aerial runway
I thinks a bit too much
Can I tackle it at my age?
I'm not too sure I can
But the little fellow has no doubts
'Cos he thinks I'm supergran
Rope ladders! - Can I climb them
I've really got my doubts
But 'Come on nanny - you can do it'
He confidently shouts
My arthritis lessens
I forget the ache and pain
He holds my hand - the years drop off
I'm just a kid again
A cosy armchair by the fire
Is not the life for me
No knitting and no crocheting
Or watching the TV.
No! I'm off to the local line dance club
Where the music's just begun
And I raise my glass and kick my heels
For I'm sixty-eight years young.

Irene Beattie

MY CAR

The sun it is shining, I'll get out the car,
Just down to the shops, it's not very far.
I wave to a neighbour, she's jealous I'm sure,
But I've driven a car since the days of the war.
I look in the mirror, there's nothing in sight.
I keep to the kerb, then shudder with fright,
There's a lorry behind me, it's too big for me,
It dirties my windscreen, I almost can't see.
I'm too old to drive, my children all said,
If I hadn't my car, I might well be dead.
I can't walk so far, arthritis they say,
But while I've got wheels I can live day by day.
If the young ones don't like it their jeers I don't heed,
I travel along, and do my own speed.
A cheeky young driver gave a rude sign,
He knew perfectly well the road right was mine.
I'll park the car here, what does it say?
No parking I think, well I won't stay all day.
What's that on my windscreen, a ticket I see,
They cannot do this to a War Horse like me.
This cannot be right, if they think I will pay,
They've another think coming, I'll throw it away.
I reach my front door with a sigh of relief,
The dent on the wing is beyond my belief.
The gate-post is damaged, what will they say,
Before it is noticed, I'll put it away.

Vera Parsonage

Don't Get Old . . . Get Bold

Why do we think old folk are dumb?
Surely, this only applies to some!

Why do we think old is frail?
Surely, not all are grey and stale?

Why do we assume 65 is over the hill?
Surely, life is better than any kind of pill?

Why do we feel old is vulnerable, or weak?
Surely, most are independent and able to speak?

Why do we believe life is over, when old?
You can't write someone off, just 'cause they're bald!

Why not bring retirement in line with life?
Make a retirement age 101 for the man, 99 for the wife?

Why give up? Celebrate good old age!
Send them back to work - to earn a good old wage!

Debra Neale

GOLDEN YEARS

People used to dread 'Old age'
It often meant despair
Of tying to cope alone
When no-one seemed to care.

These days there is a deal of help
To help folk live at home,
Carers, home helps, meals on wheels
Friendly voices on the 'phone.

Senior Citizens, a moaning lot?
I have not found them so
Making the best of everything
With their limited cash flow.

Holidays abroad often the norm
For those who are still able
Others many pleasures find
With CDs, videos, TV-Cable.

A special rate for many things
A pass to board a bus,
Experience of a lifetime
There is no need for fuss.

People are living longer
Life is easier today, after
Long years of striving, saving
A percentage of their pay.

Good health is necessary
For those who do and dare,
For the world's your oyster wheeling
In your battery driven chair.

Plenty of clubs and meetings
Dancing, bingo, bridge, golf, too,
Making life a pleasure
Celebrating age anew.

So celebrate the golden years
Making the most of them
Machines have taken off the stain
Housework need not be a pain . . .
Let's have a pizza once again . . .

Joan Heybourn

HERE AND NOW

How often do we ask 'Why was
I so foolish? Why was I not
clever?'
How many times do we ask
'Why was I so weak? Why
Was I not stronger?'
Alas the past is only for
learning, the future is
still to arrive.
Whatever your circumstances
Rise up fight your battle
Here and now
Whatever your circumstances
Win your success. Here and now
Whatever your circumstances
Enjoy your happiness
Here and now.

Alice Polley

FORTUNE'S PATHWAY

I'm following the leaders those who
always win,
Being one of life's failures to me
Is such a sin,
Fight the good fight win your
way up front now,
It's not the past that matters,
But the gift of the present to
allow,
Bring out the hidden talents that's
Been lurking from the past,
Fetch out your skills to make
your fortune cast,
Shining forth the golden light
In everything you do,
Showing the world this is
Truly - you,
Being a shadow is not anymore
You are now coming forward
Taking the floor,
If the pen be your fortune
Write away so free,
Then you will see the end
results,
From the powers that be.

Denise Frost

THE INHERITANCE

When Jenny came from the station
holding a brand new Smith
she was met with approbation
from all her kin and kith.

There were uncles, there were cousins,
sisters, aunts and brothers,
nephews, nieces in their dozens,
and a host of others.

Crowding round the little creature,
loud were their cries of joy.
They examined every feature:
'Oh, what a lovely boy!'

'But look at that,' somebody said,
'How strangely it appears,
He's got our Jackie's shape of head
and cousin Josie's ears.'

'He's got ginger hair like Lucy
and such a funny nose -
it's a richly-red retroussé -
it's just like Uncle Joe's.'

Then Jeremy looked at Jenny
and said 'Calamity,
I'll bet a pound to a penny
they'll blame all that on me!'

Eric Ferguson

THE SILENT WAVE

Watching a wave crash,
With such force upon a beach.
Makes any attempt to stand,
On the sand out of reach.

If you close your eyes for a moment,
You can almost hear it breathe.
As it goes out just as fast,
The silence is hard to believe.

Mary-Ann Adams

OUR GOLDEN

The years have flown
we've made it, dear -
our memories a breeze
with space and time,
ghostly echoes
of tears and laughter
like tinkling bells -
they're yours and mine.

Shall we dance a
light fandango -
shall we stand
and search the stars
for halcyon days
of yesteryear -
shall we tell that
Man on Mars

To tell old Man Moon
'coming out of hiding' -
romance us like
he used to do -
Let's have a
Golden Celebration
and tell the world
our love's still true.

Let's hit the heights
in outer-space -
relive love's memories
yet again -
return to Earth
on love's own rainbow -
Let's have a Golden Wedding Day!

Mary Skelton

HAPPY BIRTHDAY MARIE

Happy birthday Marie luv
You're fifty-five today
It's a day that's special
Hip hip, hip hip, hooray

Enjoy these happy greetings
They're full of birthday cheer
Only once in your lifetime
Will this special day, be here

Your hair is not quite silver
It's simply tinted grey
I still think of you, as the shy young girl
I married yesterday

Just like the rarest wines
Which get better, as they mature
A special category you are placed
Of this I am quite sure

It is a day that's special
'Cos you are special too
Enjoy your fifty-fifth birthday
With love, from me, to you.

Dennis N Davies

I AM NOT GROWING OLD

Some people say that I am growing old -
an old lady, in one sense this is so very true,
But it is only this earthly shell growing frail
and about that there is nothing that I can do

Though I may try to make this earthly shell
last a little longer yet it will fade away
dust returns to dust, and earth to earth,
unless Jesus comes first to take me to everlasting day

Then transformed in His glorious likeness
you shall see me in my most beautiful dress
'A robe of glory,' like Himself Divine
Transformed in His image of perfect righteousness

A perfect body in which death can never come
I'll walk the glorious streets of Heaven above
and prove to you that I am not growing old
But rejoicing in everlasting life through Jesus' love

I am not growing old but growing in His grace
Because His spirit lives within my soul
Moment by moment I am kept in His great love
Which redeems and sanctifies and makes whole

Then the glorious day when I shall see His face
and behold His Glory on Heaven's shore
The dearest face of Him who loves me so
Whose wondrous love fills my soul more and more

Everlasting life with no-one growing old
Rejoicing with our loved ones gone before
I thank Thee my Saviour Redeemer and my King
Help us all to love Thee, worship and adore.

Doris L Middleditch

GETTING OLD TOGETHER

The evenings dark, the nights so cold
No longer young, just getting old
The clock allows no time to spare
Just ticks away on the shelf over there.

The dog looks lazily at the dying fire
His nose pressed against the fireguard wire
Dreaming of walks and romps in the grass
Like his master his running days are past.

Their life goes on for man and friend
When will it stop, where will it end
Fond memories shared between these two
Now neither have too much to do.

The clock still ticking on the shelf
Man must survive, must help himself
Things may be bad, may even be better
For this elderly man and his red setter.

Francis E Cockram

MEMORIES WITHIN ME

Life to me is living it
I learnt that as a child,
I cherished every day I lived
The rage of war was wild.

I was witness to the anger,
The tears the telegrams brought,
On bended knee I prayed for peace
And for all of those who fought.

As I lived my in-between years
Feeling neither here or there,
Bored with my childhood games
Early teen years never seemed fair.

It's a passing time we all go through
It's the changing of our ways,
With hopeful dreams for our future years
As we live our present days.

As I look back through all my years
Many memories I have made,
I have framed them all within my heart
So they will never fade.

Barbara E Flanagan

INFORMATION

We hope you have enjoyed reading this book - and that you will continue to enjoy it in the coming years.

If you like reading and writing poetry drop us a line, or give us a call, and we'll send you a free information pack.

Write to :-
Arrival Press Information
1-2 Wainman Road
Woodston
Peterborough
PE2 7BU
(01733) 230762